weir
v

Stuart McLean

Crombie Jardine
Publishing Limited
Office 2
3 Edgar Buildings
George Street
Bath
BA1 2FJ

www.crombiejardine.com

First published in 2009 by
Crombie Jardine Publishing Limited

ISBN 978-1-906051-29-7

Written by Stuart McLean

Artwork by Polawat Darapong

Typesetting and cover design by
Matrix Media Services, Chichester, West Sussex

Printed in the UK by
CPI William Clowes Beccles NR34 7TL

CONTENTS

SITES THAT DIDN'T QUITE MAKE THE HIT LIST

Introduction

As I write, there are 162,042,117,562 websites on the internet. Of these sites, 161,983,424,031 can certainly be considered to be strange. But there are far fewer that are truly weird and even fewer that are what-on-earth-is-that-all-about-weird. This little book brings together the weirdest of these weird sites for your amusement. When visiting the sites you will meet some rich, ugly people who desperately want to marry you, you will have the opportunity to join The Interplanetary Society for the Hard of Thinking and you will be shown how to send a plague of wasps to 'destroy' the websites that you hate. So, power up that old cathode-ray tube and get surfing!

Notes

Due to the constant use of the letter 'w' every time someone types a website name into their browser, there is now a worldwide shortage of 'w's. Because of this we have not included the 'www' at the start of the websites listed in this book. Most of the time you can reach a site without the 'www.' but if a site doesn't load, try adding 'www.' to the start of the website name.

At the moment none of the sites listed contain pornographic material, though some may contain mild nudity and/or slightly bad language. However, websites do change over time so, as always on the internet, surf with caution. Please note also that specific examples mentioned for sites may well have been updated by the time you view them, but the weirdness factor of the site will doubtless remain!

For more weirdness visit:
Weird-Websites.info
Your Password to reach the Secret Pages
is: I-Am-Weird

Stuart McLean
2009

Site Name	alMost Haunted
Category	Spooky Things
Weirdness	
Website	ghost-pictures.org

the weird bits

If you've never believed in ghosts before you will probably want to change your mind after visiting this bizarre site. It apparently features genuine, scientifically proven photos including a "Retrospective haunting, where the ghost of Elvis Presley travelled into the past, to serenade Neil Armstrong as he landed on the moon." Closer to home in the UK, there are a number of photos of the nudist ghost colony that haunts Glasgow Necropolis. Also look out for the ghost of Marilyn Monroe singing *Happy Birthday* for Bill Clinton...

Site Name	Marry an Ugly Millionaire
Category	Lovey Dovey Stuff
Weirdness	
Website	marry-an-ugly-millionaire-online-dating-agency.com

Having trouble finding Mr or Mrs Right? Always in debt? Massive overdraft? Solve all your problems by marrying an ugly millionaire. Lord Smythe-Smythe may be to your liking. He's worth £22m and says, "Life would not be complete without a morning ride on Old Ben." (One should explain that when one talks about Old Ben one means one's favourite horse and not one's Head Gardener, who is also called Old Ben. Though, to honest, Old Ben is a very good snogger; the gardener, not the horse.)

weird websites

Site Name	Net Disaster
Category	Crazed Fun
Weirdness	
Website	netdisaster.com

the weird bits

Pissed off with Google? Fed up with Yahoo? Destroy them! That's right! With Net Disaster you can take a chain saw to any site and just obliterate it completely. Or why not let loose a nasty swarm of wasps or a group of dinosaurs to do the annihilation? This incredibly innovative site will provide hours of destructive fun. It's just a pity it can't really harm those annoying sites!

weird websites

Site Name	notMENSA
Category	Intellectual
Weirdness	
Website	not-mensa.com

16

the weird bits

This is great; the website for The Interplanetary Society for the Hard of Thinking.

To quote the site, "Congratulations you have somehow managed to navigate through the cluttered internet and found our site. While you're here why not waste your time on our pointless IQ Tests – just to prove that you really do have the brains of a hedgehog."

My test result:
"IQ: 58 (Medically speaking, you're lucky to be conscious). Personality: You don't seem to have one. Keep friendly with your cat – she's the only one that likes you."

weird websites

Site Name	Fugly
Category	Ugly People
Weirdness	
Website	fugly.net

the weird bits

Most people are simply unremarkable. The few who are stunningly beautiful and two standard deviations from the norm enjoy attention, acclaim, and recognition. Through no effort of their own, they enjoy the privileges of beauty. But they're not alone... there are thousands born under much the same star, but two standard deviations from the norm in the opposite direction. This site is an attempt to rectify that injustice, to give the ugly people their fifteen minutes of fame. Uglies, we love you – though maybe not a lot.

Site Name	Totally Absurd Inventions
Category	Mad Inventors
Weirdness	
Website	totallyabsurd.com

the weird bits

This site explores the funnier side of our inventive spirit by unveiling America's Goofiest Patents. There's the Alarm Fork which reduces obesity by forcing people to eat slowly. The rules: you can only eat when the fork gives you the green light. That's right, once you've shovelled some food into your mouth, the fork sensors cue the fork to emit a red light. And you know what that means: STOP! Now wait... tick, tick, tick... ding! Green light, take a bite. This site is truly a mad inventor's paradise.

weird websites

Site Name	The Brick Testament
Category	Holy Weird
Weirdness	
Website	thebricktestament.com

This is the Bible according to Lego... The Brick Testament is the world's largest, most comprehensive illustrated Bible with over 3,600 illustrations that retell more than 300 stories from the Bible – all done in beautiful 3D Lego bricks. Wonderfully illustrated stories such as *The Last Supper* and *The Burning Bush* are all acted out with yellow and red bricks – with a little help from a felt tip pen and a few bits of felt here and there.

Site Name	Insult Generator
Category	Verbal Abuse
Weirdness	
Website	insult-generator.com

If you are married you probably won't need this site. However, if you don't have a 'significant other' to foul mouth you then let this site tell you things like, "Ye've goat a face like a wet nicht lookin' for a dry mornin'." and "You're three tassels short of a sporran." If you really want to feel insulted, keep pressing the 'Insult' button for more verbal abuse.

weird websites

Site Name	Free Rice
Category	Rice for Words
Weirdness	
Website	freerice.com

the weird bits

Play the word game and help starving children! Yes – that's really the deal. You'll be shown a word and four possible definitions – all you have to do is select the correct definition. Every time you get an answer right, twenty grains of rice are donated to the United Nations World Food Program (and paid for by advertisers on the site). At the time of writing, over 20 billion grains of rice have been donated. What are you waiting for?

weird websites

Site Name	Humans for Sale
Category	Self Doubt
Weirdness	
Website	humanforsale.com

the weird bits

Have you been thinking about putting yourself up for sale lately? Ever wondered how much money you would make on the open human market? This bizarre site will place a value on your life based on a variety of factors. The criteria used include athletic ability, level of education, income, amount of exercise you take, weight and sense of humour. Give it a try and see if you're worth more than the cost of this book.

Site Name	Headless Historicals
Category	Gruesome History
Weirdness	
Website	headlesshistoricals.com

the weird bits

See dolls of famous historical figures such as Anne Boleyn, Mary Stuart and Thomas More... headless.

Headless Historicals are dolls inspired by people throughout history who died in rather horrible ways. Each doll is dressed as their personality might have appeared at the peak of their success, while their bodies display the manner in which they died. Why not buy one for your display cabinet? That will certainly be a conversation starter when great Aunt Agatha calls round for tea...

weird websites

Site Name	Wild Recipes
Category	Fatal Foods
Weirdness	
Website	wildrecipes.com

the weird bits

Here is a site that brings you the strangest foods from around the world. Dare to impress your friends with delights such as Cheddar Coffee, Choco Dogs and Scrambled Brains. As the title suggests, recipes are supplied for this weird selection of foods so there's no excuse for not giving them a try. Just make sure you have a stomach pump to hand when you do experiment! (Alternatively, get your partner to try them first.)

weird websites

Site Name	Baby Name Generator
Category	Name Game
Weirdness	
Website	baby-names.name

the weird bits

Choosing a new baby name is not easy. You can spend weeks scouring books and making up your short-list. But, of course, your partner has created a completely different list. Then the big day arrives, baby is here but still no name... That's when you panic. Two days later, in desperation, you call the poor little newcomer something really weird like Jasemie or Nharobee and the child is scarred for life. Well, your worries are over! Let this site choose the perfect name – completely randomly.

weird websites

Site Name	Riddles Online
Category	Tease Brainers
Weirdness	
Website	riddles-online.com

the weird bits

Riddles galore (ranging from easy to difficult, word, logic, maths, funny, kids, birthday, etc.) plus brain twisters and What Am I?

Q: True or False?
The following sentence is false.
The preceding sentence is true.
Are these sentences true or false?

A: Neither, its a paradox.
If the first is true, then the second must be false, which makes the first false.

weird websites

Site Name	Marry Your Pet
Category	Petosexual
Weirdness	
Website	marryyourpet.com

the weird bits

So you've found your partner, but you've just one little problem... Not only does he shit on the carpet and have abominable table manners, but he's an animal, with feathers, fur, scales or whatever.

But who cares? What does it matter that he has an overabundance of legs, eats flies, or has to hibernate during winter? The important thing is that you adore him. So go on, if you really love him and you're willing to commit for life, it really is time for you to... marry your pet!

weird websites

Site Name	Morphases
Category	Pulling Faces
Weirdness	
Website	morphases.com

the weird bits

This is a fun site that allows you to manipulate human faces to make them look like those old identikit pictures you used to see on things like *Crimewatch*. Yes, it's all a bit pointless but then so is most of the internet. Once you've completed your very own creation, you can save your ugly mug for future visitors to marvel at. The perfect site for budding Frankensteins!

weird websites

Site Name	All About Frogs
Category	Croak Croak
Weirdness	
Website	allaboutfrogs.org

the weird bits

Everything you always wanted to know about frogs but were just too embarrassed to ask... Learn about raising tadpoles, feeding your frog and dealing with icky bugs. Be sure to visit the frog doctor to find out what to do when Mr Frog gets sick. If you want more details about a specific type of frog, then check out the species care sheets for in-depth information. There's even a great section with suggestions for naming your pet frog!

Then there's always:
cuisine-france.com/recipes/frog-legs.htm

Site Name	Worst Jobs
Category	Career Calamity
Weirdness	
Website	worst-jobs.com

Many of us hate our jobs, but Worst Jobs will make your job seem like a picnic and your career a yellow-brick-road of opportunity. On this site the worst jobs are revealed in all their horrid detail. Take, for instance, the Slaughterhouse Operative: "You have the fine job of cutting the heads off chickens and other animals. As the animals get bigger, they get progressively more difficult to kill and there's much more blood. Keep your hatchet sharp and try not to get affected by their screams for mercy."

Site Name	Your Not Me
Category	Someone Else
Weirdness	
Website	yournotme.com

the weird bits

Like most paranoid schizophrenics, I often think that I'm someone else. When I found this site I thought, from its title, that it would help me discover my own unique identity. But when I did a search for 'Stuart McLean' it told me that there were 145 people with that name in the UK. 145! The problem I have now is that I'm not sure which one of them I am. Oh well, at least I'm glad I'm not John Smith – there were 11,782 of him!!

Site Name	Strictly No Photography
Category	Candid Camera
Weirdness	
Website	strictlynophotography.com

the weird bits

Strictly No Photography is a photo-sharing site for photographs taken where you are not allowed to take them. From the inside of the Kremlin to Kensington Palace, from art galleries to war zones. On the site you can see a variety of things you've always wanted to see, mostly because you're not supposed to. There are pictures that range from the rather ordinary to the profound. Whatever the content or the quality, though, each one stands as a little piece of art in itself, as a small expression of personal liberty.

Site Name	National Novel Writing Month
Category	Write Weird
Weirdness	
Website	nanowrimo.org

the weird bits

Do you think you could write a novel in just one month? To quote the site, "National Novel Writing Month is a fun, seat-of-your-pants approach to novel writing. Participants begin on the 1st of November. The goal is to write a 50,000-word novel by midnight, November 30." Because of the limited writing window, the only thing that matters in NaNoWriMo is output. It's all about quantity, not quality. The kamikaze approach forces you to lower your expectations, take risks, and write whenever you have a spare moment. Visit the site and take the challenge!

weird websites

Site Name	Oddee
Category	Odd Oddities
Weirdness	
Website	oddee.com

the weird bits

It seems like all the oddities of the world have come together in one very small space... Included on this site are some unfortunate car names. It's not surprising that the Mazda La Puta is not popular in Spain, where La Puta (in Spanish), means 'The Whore'. Another story tells of a 64-year-old Thai man called Ngoc. Apparently this poor chap has not had a night's sleep for over 30 years. In spite of 11,700 consecutive sleepless nights, medical examinations have shown him to be fit and healthy. Visit now for more strange stories.

weird websites

Site Name	Global Rich List
Category	Dollariffic
Weirdness	
Website	globalrichlist.com

the weird bits

There are 6,602,224,175 people in the world. Some are richer than you. Some are poorer than you. But where exactly do you sit on the richness scale? Here's your chance to find out. Just visit the site, enter your annual income into the box and hit the 'Show me the Money' button. Instantly you'll discover how many people are richer than you. At this precise moment, for example, if you earn £25,000 per year then you are the 85,565,218 richest person in the world! Feel good now?

Site Name	The Spam Letters
Category	Spam Spam Spam Spam
Weirdness	
Website	thespamletters.com

the weird bits

We all get spam from time to time and most of us hate it with a vengeance – except Jon. Jon doesn't delete the 30 spam emails he gets each day; he writes back and with amusing effect. Whether it's an Algerian wanting to put £98.7 billion into his bank account or someone selling Viagra, Jon writes back and writes again and again and again until the poor sods can't take it any more! Read Jon's emails and split your sides laughing.

weird websites

Site Name	Human Clock
Category	Time Machine
Weirdness	
Website	humanclock.com

the weird bits

Forget boring old mechanical and digital clocks; this clock features real people from all around the world. It is made up of thousands of photos, mainly contributed by visitors. Each picture is unique and often very funny. Every minute a new picture is displayed. When I looked just now, 17:35 featured a young lad sitting on the lavvie and 10:44 showed the time written in snow in Milan. This is one clock you'll never grow tired of watching and you might even submit your own photo and get your one minute of fame.

weird websites

Site Name	Verbotomy
Category	Wordimakupsees
Weirdness	
Website	verbotomy.com

the weird bits

This site is all about creating new words. Every day a new definition and matching cartoon are shown. Your challenge is to create a word that matches the definition. Then you can vote for other authors' words to help select the winning verboticism. For example, 'mepathy' was the winning word for 'To seek appreciation, support, and/or love by trying to get people to feel sorry for you. Someone who believes that if you don't feel sorry for them, you do not love them.'

Site Name	String Figures
Category	Dumb Things to Do
Weirdness	
Website	stringfigure.com

the weird bits

Here's everything you wanted to know about string figures but were too bored to ask. Quote, "String figures have been found in almost all of the cultures of the world and new ones continue to be created. Most people remember the games of Cat's Cradle, Cup and Saucer and Jacob's Ladder but there are thousands more. Intricate geometric patterns are revealed as the movement of the hands dance to a rhythm of motion. A universal motion in time and space." Ho hum... Is it just me or have you fallen asleep too?

weird websites

Site Name	Tech Tales
Category	Dumb People
Weirdness	
Website	techtales.com

the weird bits

Techies are renowned for being a little dumb but it seems their customers are dumber. Example:

Techie: "Hello, May I help you?"

Customer: "This is my third call and I still can't get connected."

Techie: "So what's the trouble?"

Customer: "It's just not connecting. I don't know why."

Techie: "Well, let's check again. Can you go back to your desktop?"

Customer: "Oh! Maybe that's the problem. I don't have a desktop. The computer is on the floor."

weird websites

Site Name	Why did the chicken...
Category	Road Runners
Weirdness	
Website	Whydidthechickencross theroad.com

the weird bits

So why *did* the chicken cross the road? On this site you'll hear the outspoken opinions of world leaders and other celebrities on this topical question. Al Gore claims, "I fight for the chickens and I am fighting for the chickens right now. I will not give up on the chickens crossing the road! I will fight for the chickens and I will not disappoint them. Did I mention that I invented roads?"

weird websites

Site Name	Horoscope Online
Category	Your Future
Weirdness	
Website	horoscope-online.org

the weird bits

The world is changing rapidly and with each day come new innovations in science, technology and cake decorating. Sometimes the world just seems too confusing; it now takes a maths degree just to make a cup of tea! More changes have taken place in the last five years than in the previous 500. No wonder more and more people are turning to astrology to make sense of their future and to find stability in this turbulent world. This site doesn't just tell you your future, it creates it for you!

weird websites

Site Name	Reincarnation Station
Category	I'm a Duck
Weirdness	
Website	reincarnationstation.com

the weird bits

Reincarnation, literally meaning 'to be made flesh again', is a doctrine or metaphysical belief that argues that some essential part of a living being survives death to be reborn in a new body. Whether you believe this or not will definitely be influenced by your visit to Reincarnation Station. After a question and answer session based on how I have lived my present life so far, the site told me that I'll come back as a duck – which rather pleases me!

Site Name	Silly Walks Generator
Category	Pythonesque
Weirdness	
Website	sillywalksgenerator.com

the weird bits

A must-visit site for Monty Python fans and anyone who's obsessed with silly walks. This is sure to provide minutes of endless fun... Do read the small print – it's the funniest part of the site: "When you submit any contribution... you agree... a perpetual, royalty-free, non-exclusive, sub-licensable right and license to use, reproduce, modify, adapt, publish, translate, create derivative works from, distribute, perform, play, make available to the public, and exercise all copyright and publicity rights with respect to your contribution... " Blah, blah, boring blah!!

weird websites

Site Name	Talk Like a Pirate
Category	Arrr Me Hearties.
Weirdness	
Website	talklikeapirate.com

the weird bits

What do you celebrate on the 19th of September? No, it's not the day you traditionally buy your Christmas tree and cover the house in a million watts of electric bulbs; it's International Talk Like a Pirate Day. It all started when two guys had a fun idea which then snowballed and now the whole world is talking like pirates once a year. So get ye down to the site ye land lubber where ye can find the finest pirate booty and study up on the pirate lingo – ohhh arrr.

weird websites

Site Name	Worst City
Category	Get the Hell Out of There!
Weirdness	
Website	worst-city.com

the weird bits

The world is very, very big. There are some wonderful places on its surface: fabulous, sun-kissed beaches with miles and miles of golden sands; fantastic mountains with beautiful crystal steams cascading down into tropical paradises. There are also some bloody horrendous cities populated by a subculture of thugs and gangsters and places where a rat could feed a family for a week. Sadly this website is about the latter locations. Here you will discover some of the most vile and violent places to live. So visit now but be prepared to be shocked.

Site Name	The 39 Dollar Experiment
Category	Internet Begging
Weirdness	
Website	the39dollarexperiment.com

the weird bits

What happened when Tom sent off 100 letters to companies asking for free stuff? Tom had $39 and a choice: buy food, lose the money at a casino table or buy 100 stamps and try to persuade companies to give him some freebies. Tom chose the third option. The result? Some very witty begging letters. But did he get the goodies? Visit the site to find out.

Site Name	Geeky Gadgets
Category	Boys' Toys
Weirdness	
Website	geeky-gadgets.com

the weird bits

News and reviews, on technology, gadgets and everything geeky. The website is updated on a daily basis to bring you up-to-the-minute news on geeky gadgets and other cool stuff. It showcases the world's most expensive toy car; a crazy little plaything that's encrusted with more than 2,700 diamonds and is valued at $140,000. It was made by Hot Wheels to commemorate the production of their 4-billionth toy car.

Site Name	Lunch Clock
Category	Stealing Time
Weirdness	
Website	lunchclock.com

the weird bits

We all have them – those long, long work days when we wish we could steal an extra ten minutes or so for lunch. Well now you can do just that whenever you wish! With Lunch Clock you simply set the amount of time you normally have for lunch and the extra amount of time you want. After that the clock will speed up before lunch then slow down during lunch to allow that extra long break. What could be simpler?

weird websites

Site Name	Funny Poems
Category	Rhyme Thyme
Weirdness	
Website	funny-poems.biz

the weird bits

A great collection of funny poems organised by poet and theme. Here's an old favourite:

The Crocodile by Lewis Carroll

How doth the little crocodile
Improve his shining tail,
And pour the waters of the Nile,
On every golden scale!

How cheerfully he seems to grin!
How neatly spread his claws,
And welcomes little fishes in,
With gently smiling jaws!

weird websites

Site Name	International Association of Fully Clothed Nudes
Category	No Naughty Bits
Weirdness	
Website	international-association-of-fully-clothed-nudes.com

the weird bits

The International Association of Fully Clothed Nudes may well seem like a contradiction in terms! How can you be clothed and nude? Well, nudism is not possible for everyone who wishes to be free of the restriction of clothes. There are many reasons why potential nudists can't fulfil their dreams: they may be too shy to be seen nude in public; they might live in a region where it's too cold for nudism to be practical; or they may simply be too damn ugly to appear naked in public! Visit the site and join the club!

weird websites

Site Name	Ghost Stories
Category	Don't Read at Bedtime
Weirdness	
Website	Ghost-stories.net

the weird bits

A collection of both true and fictional spooky stories plus a haunting of ghostly poems. The site also features ghostly items that have been sold on eBay – one of these is a lump of ghost-poo. Yes! The seller claims she lives in a haunted house. One night strange noises suddenly erupted from the bathroom. The door vibrated wildly. Finally it stopped. When she went in she discovered the ghostly poo on the floor. She hopes that by selling the poo the ghost will leave her in peace.

weird websites

Site Name	Subservient Chicken
Category	Eat with Chips
Weirdness	
Website	subservientchicken.com

the weird bits

Tell the chicken to jump, fall, talk, kiss, run, die or whatever and it will obey your commands. The site seems to have been commissioned by Burger King, which is rather irritating, but otherwise it's a good bit of clean fun. Tell the subservient chicken to be free range and see what it does.

weird websites

Site Name	Fairies World
Category	Fairy Good
Weirdness	
Website	fairiesworld.com

the weird bits

Sadly, in this age of technology, very few people believe in fairies but this site will certainly win a few converts. It started humbly in 1999 as a three-page promotion for the fabulous fairy artist Myrea Pettit. From there it has grown into a massive website, providing fairy facts, fairy folklore, fairy names, fairy games, creative and fantasy art, education material, fairy products and even details of fairy festivals. Take some time to enjoy Myrea's amazing fairy artwork.

Site Name	Find a Grave
Category	Afterlife Housing Estate
Weirdness	
Website	findagrave.com

the weird bits

At first Find a Grave seems a bit gruesome – probably because it actually is! But the site not only gives details of the last resting places of the rich and famous; it's also a useful tool for researching your ancestry and has access to 20 million grave records. A search for 'Stuart McLean' came back with "Gunner Stuart McLean of the Royal Field Artillery. He died in action, aged 25, on 22nd August 1917 and is buried in West-Vlaanderen, Belgium." Made me feel rather sad reading that!

Site Name	Sketch Swap
Category	Doodle Bug
Weirdness	
Website	sketchswap.com

the weird bits

If you love to doodle or if you're an Etchosketch fan with hours of time to waste... you will love this site. It's a fairly simple concept: create a drawing and it will be shown to another visitor on the site. Meanwhile, you get to see the drawing done by some random person who's probably as equally boring as you are... Somewhat strangely addictive.

Site Name	Wedding Betting
Category	Blissful Odds
Weirdness	
Website	weddingbetting.com

the weird bits

On this site you're shown a photo of a pair of newly weds and are told a little about them. Then you're invited to speculate on how long they will stay married...

Here's what it said about Joy and Michael: "Joy and Michael met in graduate school. They dated for 18 months before getting married. Both are teachers. They are both geniuses, but had to have Michael's stepmother arrested on their wedding day in front of the entire wedding party."
I'd give them six months max!

weird websites

Site Name	Death Clock
Category	Final Countdown
Weirdness	
Website	deathclock.com

the weird bits

Okay, so we all know that we're going to die sometime. But would you really like to know when, to the precise second? Would you care for a clock on your computer screen that ticks down the seconds until your demise? That is exactly what Death Clock gives you; the final countdown! Apparently, I have 1,513,482,342 seconds left – think I'll go and take an aspirin!

weird websites

Site Name	Where's George
Category	Fast Buck
Weirdness	
Website	wheresgeorge.com

the weird bits

Do you ever wonder where that paper money in your pocket has been, or where it will go next? This is the place to find out. It's a fascinating site that was set up to track $1 around the US (and the world). Users enter the serial number of their money and their location. The site gives back details of where the money has been – even showing a map of its travels. Fascinating fun, even if it is American.

Site Name	Cow Abduction
Category	UFcOw
Weirdness	
Website	cowabduction.com

the weird bits

It's a very serious problem! Countless cows (529,024 to be exact, the last time I checked) are disappearing from farms and shopping malls – mostly in California but also elsewhere. This site not only highlights the problem, it provides authentic reports, photos and videos of aliens stealing our bovine friends. It shows how one farmer has had to fit antlers to his 700 cows to disguise them as deer in an effort to stop them being stolen by aliens. Help stamp out cow abduction by visiting the site now!

weird websites

Site Name	Book Crossing
Category	Lost and Found
Weirdness	
Website	bookcrossing.com

the weird bits

What are you going to do with this book when you've finished with it? Throw it in the bin? Burn it in some Satanic ritual? Why not leave it on a train for someone else to read then follow its travels around the world on Book Crossing? These guys have come up with a terrific idea for book sharing and the website makes it fun to find out where books have been left and also to track the journeys they have made. Get sharing.

Site Name	Tomatoes Are Evil
Category	Red Alert
Weirdness	
Website	tomatoesareevil.com

the weird bits

This site is dedicated to the small percentage of the Earth's population that does not like tomatoes. We are not talking about a mild dislike or a medical allergy here; but the belief that this fruit is the 'Spawn of Satan'. Yep – whether the tomatoes are Cherry, Plum, Beef, Sun dried, Green, Organic or home grown, this site states that *all* are evil. Visit now and join the debate. Or just play the 'tomatoes are evil, take your revenge' game!

Site Name	Adopt Me
Category	Virtual Poo
Weirdness	
Website	adoptme.com

the weird bits

The problem with animals is that they crap all over the bedroom carpet and if you happen to own an elephant that can be a real nuisance. But now that everyone has a cyber life, you can adopt a virtual pet. On this site you can have dogs, cats, fish, horses, snakes and other animals. They do still poo, of course, but with your virtual pooper-scooper you can clean up without the bother or expense of calling in the carpet fitter.

weird websites

Site Name	Museum of Bad Art
Category	Art Attack
Weirdness	
Website	museumofbadart.org

the weird bits

The Museum Of Bad Art (MOBA) is the world's only museum dedicated to the collection, preservation, exhibition and celebration of bad art in all its forms and glory. The pieces in the MOBA collection range from the work of talented artists that have gone awry to works of exuberant, albeit crude, execution by artists barely in control of the brush. What they all have in common is a special quality that sets them apart in one way or another from the merely incompetent.

weird websites

Site Name	The Dialectizer
Category	Word Warping
Weirdness	
Website	rinkworks.com/dialect

the weird bits

Create a hilarious parody of your favourite website, story or poem with The Dialectizer. With one press of the button you can change a site or text into Redneck, Jive, Cockney, Elmer Fudd, Swedish Chef, Moron, or Pig Latin. For example, using Elmer Fudd, 'Mary had a little lamb. Her face was white as snow' transforms into 'Mawy had a wittwe wamb. Hew fwace was white as swow.' Hours of moronic fun to be had here...

weird websites

Site Name	Spot the Duck
Category	Duck Cam
Weirdness	
Website	Spot-the-Duck.com

the weird bits

Spot was first sighted at Loch Lomond in August 2001. Scientists are totally bewildered as to what type of duck he can be – there are no other ducks of this type anywhere in the world! One theory is that he's a prehistoric duck related to the dinosaur. Spot has become an overnight phenomenon – a bigger sensation than the Loch Ness Monster itself. Tourists from all over the world are rushing to the loch in the hope of catching a glimpse of Spot. Now you can see him too – if you are patient and lucky.

weird websites

Site Name	End of the Internet
Category	The End
Weirdness	
Website	end-of-the-internet.info

This is the very last page on the internet – there is nothing else to follow. No more links, no further pop-ups, no more adverts. It's now time to switch off your computer and get a life!

Sites that didn't quite make the hit list...

nycgarbage.com : Get your piece of NY trash.

horrorfind.com : Everything dark and evil on the web.

free-view-webcams.net : Cams from around the world.

songfacts.com : Find out where lyrics come from.

privateislandsonline.com : Treat yourself to a tropical paradise.

sudftw.com : The Weather Randomizer and more.

sites that didn't quite make the hit list

funbureau.com : Explores the missing sock phenomenon.

googlefight.com : Start a fight between two words or people.

theflatearthsociety.org : Find out why the Earth is flat.

hsx.com : Buy shares in a movie.

skeptiseum.org : The skeptical museum of the paranormal.

humorous-free-scripts.com : Funny scripts.

geocities.com/Heartland/Plains/2144 : turn into cabbage.

geocities.com/Heartland/Bluffs/8105 : Blatant online begging.

weird websites

ericharshbarger.com/lego : Lego sculptures.

grouphug.us : Weird confessions – hug or shrug.

ultimatetaxi.com : The ultimate taxi ride.

snopes.com : A world of rumours.

text-image.com : Hours of fun with text images.

extremeironing.com : The latest danger sport – let the wife do it.

urban75.com/Punch : Punch a celebrity.

ibiblio.org/hollerin : They holler Amazing Grace.

sites that didn't quite make the hit list

workpoop.com : Calculate your poo costs.

bathroomsurvey.com : Do you perform properly?

actualaliens.com : All about alien abductions and sightings.

uglymailbox.com : That's no way to get your mail.

ipspotting.com : Get to know your IP address.

worldwidewig.co.uk : Adventures of the world wide wig.

weirdconverter.com : How many cockroaches in a T-Rex?

weird websites

cracked.com : Humour and videos.

itsawonderfulinternet.com : An internet tale.

christmas-jokes.info : Weird joke collection.

papertoys.com : Origami gone mad.

mr-lee-catcam.de : Spend a day with a cat.

freethegnomes.com : Stop gnome slavery.

crashbonsai.com : When car meets tree.

halfbakery.com : Some weird ideas.

awfulplasticsurgery.com : Celebrity surgery mishaps.

sites that didn't quite make the hit list

ourstrangeworld.net : Guide to all things odd.

clientcopia.com : Stupid quotes from customers.

allmylifeforsale.com : John sold his life.

pick-up-artists.org : How to pick up totty.

sexgage.com : Find out if you're sexy.

futureme.org : Send an email – in the future.

urinal.net : Worth a visit!

infinitecat.com : An infinity of cats.

manbehindthedoll.com : Barbie's boyfriend.

weird websites

thecuriousdreamer.com : What dreams mean.

dirtycarart.com : Art on dirty cars.

imagineaworldwithoutpaper.com : Paperless world.

funny-jokes-online.com : Joke bucket.

barcodeart.com : Wicked art.

deathonline.net : Find out about death.

manwillneverfly.com : Flight is impossible.

monitorcamera.com : Take your photo.

bermuda-triangle.org : Don't disappear.

dumbcrooks.com : Things thugs do.

funny-posters.net : Funny posters.

sites that didn't quite make the hit list

linesthataregood.com : Pick-up lines.

hatsofmeat.com : Hats made of meat!

dullmen.com : Dull Men's Club.

hencam.co.uk : See the hen lay eggs.

emotioneric.com : Eric showing emotions.

megamonalisa.com : Mona Lisa art.

thispeanutlookslikeaduck.com : It does.

r2d2translator.com : Translate to R2D2.

funnysign.com : Funny signs.

leversgame.com : Silly game.

biglongnow.com : Open doors.

papertoilet.com : Unravel in the loo.

weird websites

warninglabelgenerator.com : Create a label.

sat-gps-locate.com : Find the wife.

isthisyou.co.uk : What have you been up to?

hamsterdance.com : It's a hamster.

worldbeardchampionships.com : I could win that!

phobialist.com : What are you afraid of?

piws.org : Personal injury warning service – signs that can save your life.

deadfishcam.com : See the fishy.